Fun and Festive

SPRING CRAFTS

Flower Puppets, Bunny Masks, and Mother's Day Pop-up Cards

Randel McGee

Enslow Elementary

an imprint of

Enslow Publishers, Inc.

40 Industrial Road
Box 398
Berkeley Heights, NJ 07922
USA

http://www.enslow.com

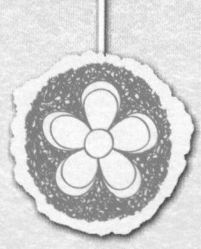

Dedicated to Emma and Lily McGee

Enslow Elementary, an imprint of Enslow Publishers, Inc.
Enslow Elementary® is a registered trademark of Enslow Publishers, Inc.

Library of Congress Cataloging-in-Publication Data

McGee, Randel.
  Fun and festive spring crafts : flower puppets, bunny masks, and Mother's Day pop-up cards / Randel McGee.
    pages cm. — (Fun and festive crafts for the seasons)
  Includes bibliographical references and index.
  Audience: Ages 8-up.
  Audience: Grades 4 to 6.
  Summary: "Includes the scientific explanation behind the spring season, a related myth, and step-by-step instructions on
    how to make eight spring-themed crafts out of various materials"— Provided by publisher.
  ISBN 978-0-7660-4318-3 — ISBN 978-1-4644-0581-5 (paperback) — ISBN 978-1-4646-1280-0 (single-user PDF) —
    ISBN (invalid) 978-0-7660-5912-2 (multi-user PDF) — ISBN 978-1-4645-1280-3 (epub)
    1. Handicraft—Juvenile literature. 2. Spring—Juvenile literature. I. Title.
  TT160.M3848 2015
  745.5—dc23

                                                    2013022079

Future editions:
Paperback ISBN: 978-1-4644-0581-5   EPUB ISBN: 978-1-4645-1280-3
Single-User PDF ISBN: 978-1-4646-1280-0   Multi-User PDF ISBN: 978-0-7660-5912-2

Printed in the United States of America

052014 Lake Book Manufacturing, Inc., Melrose Park, IL

10 9 8 7 6 5 4 3 2 1

To Our Readers: We have done our best to make sure all Internet addresses in this book were active and appropriate when we went to press. However, the author and the publisher have no control over and assume no liability for the material available on those Internet sites or on other Web sites they may link to. Any comments or suggestions can be sent by e-mail to comments@enslow.com or to the address on the back cover.

Every effort has been made to locate all copyright holders of material used in this book. If any errors or omissions have occurred, corrections will be made in future editions of this book.

♻ Enslow Publishers, Inc., is committed to printing our books on recycled paper. The paper in every book contains 10% to 30% post-consumer waste (PCW). The cover board on the outside of each book contains 100% PCW. Our goal is to do our part to help young people and the environment too!

Photo Credits: Crafts prepared by Randel McGee and p. 48; craft photography by Enslow Publishers, Inc.; Designua/Shutterstock.com, p. 5.

Cover photo: Crafts prepared by Randel McGee; photography by Enslow Publishers, Inc.

Contents

AUTHOR'S NOTE: The projects in this book were created for this particular season. However, I invite readers to be imaginative and find new ways to use the ideas in this book to create different projects of their own. Please feel free to share pictures of your work with me through www.mcgeeproductions.com. Happy crafting!

SPRING!

Demeter (Deh-MEE-ter), the Greek goddess of the harvest, had a beautiful daughter named Persephone (Per-SEFF-o-nee). Everyone loved Persephone for her cheerfulness. Hades, the king of the Underworld, wanted her for his queen.

One day, Hades captured Persephone and would not let her go. Demeter did not know what had happened to Persephone. She stopped making plants grow and searched for her lost daughter. The world became cold and the crops died. The people were cold and hungry.

Zeus, the leader of the Greek gods, knew what Hades had done and told him that he had to free Persephone so that the crops would grow again. Hades tricked Persephone into eating fruit from his garden, which forced her to spend half of the year with him. Spring became the time that Persephone returned home to her mother, and Demeter celebrated by making flowers grow.

As the Northern Hemisphere—the top half of Earth that includes North America—tilts closer to the sun, the days get longer and warmer. The vernal (spring) equinox (EE-quih-nox)

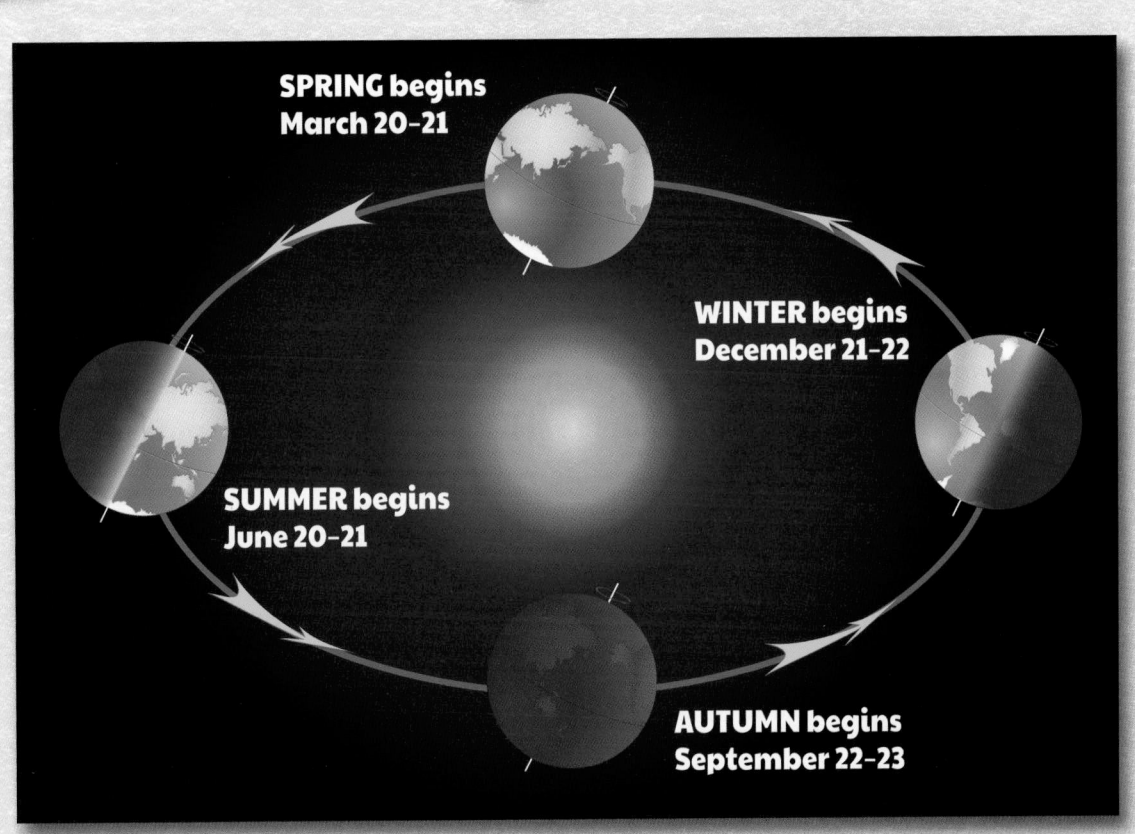

SPRING begins
March 20-21

WINTER begins
December 21-22

SUMMER begins
June 20-21

AUTUMN begins
September 22-23

is the first day of spring and is a day when the day and night hours are equal in length. March 20 is usually the vernal equinox, but the day can change due to leap years.

Spring is the time of year when the world comes alive after winter. In spring, plants sprout, trees bloom, birds build nests, and animals have babies. There are special holidays in spring, such as St. Patrick's Day, Easter, Passover, Memorial Day, Mother's Day, and Father's Day.

Growing Flower Puppet

As winter warms into spring, seeds from last summer start to sprout. The seed sends a small root into the soil to collect water and nutrients to help it grow. It sends up a little stem with a leaf to collect energy from sunshine. Soon plants push up from the ground with flower buds. Later we see the bright colors of spring and smell the sweet flowers. What do you think this flower puppet would say about spring?

What you will need:

- a 12-inch-long dowel, ¼ inch thick
- acrylic paints
- paintbrush
- air-drying clay
- pencil or permanent markers
- craft foam—different colors
- scissors
- a 16-ounce plastic drinking cup
- glue
- a wooden bead with a ¼-inch-wide hole (optional)

WHAT TO DO:

1. Paint the dowel green. Let it dry.

#1

2. Make a ball of clay about the size of a cherry and stick it at one end of the dowel. Let it dry in place.

#3

3. Paint the clay ball and let it dry. Draw a face on the ball with permanent markers.

4. Draw flower petals and leaves on craft foam with a pencil or marker. Cut them out. Cut out a small hole in the middle of each piece so you can stick the dowel through.

#4

5. (a) Trace around the open end of the plastic cup to make a circle on another piece of craft foam. (b) Draw an asterisk in the center of the circle as shown. Cut out the circle. Cut the center into "slices of pie." **Note:** Do not cut all the way to the edge of the circle.

#5a

#5b

6. Glue the petals around the flower head by the dowel. Glue the leaves along the dowel. Glue the circle of craft foam over the top of the plastic cup. Let everything dry.

#6

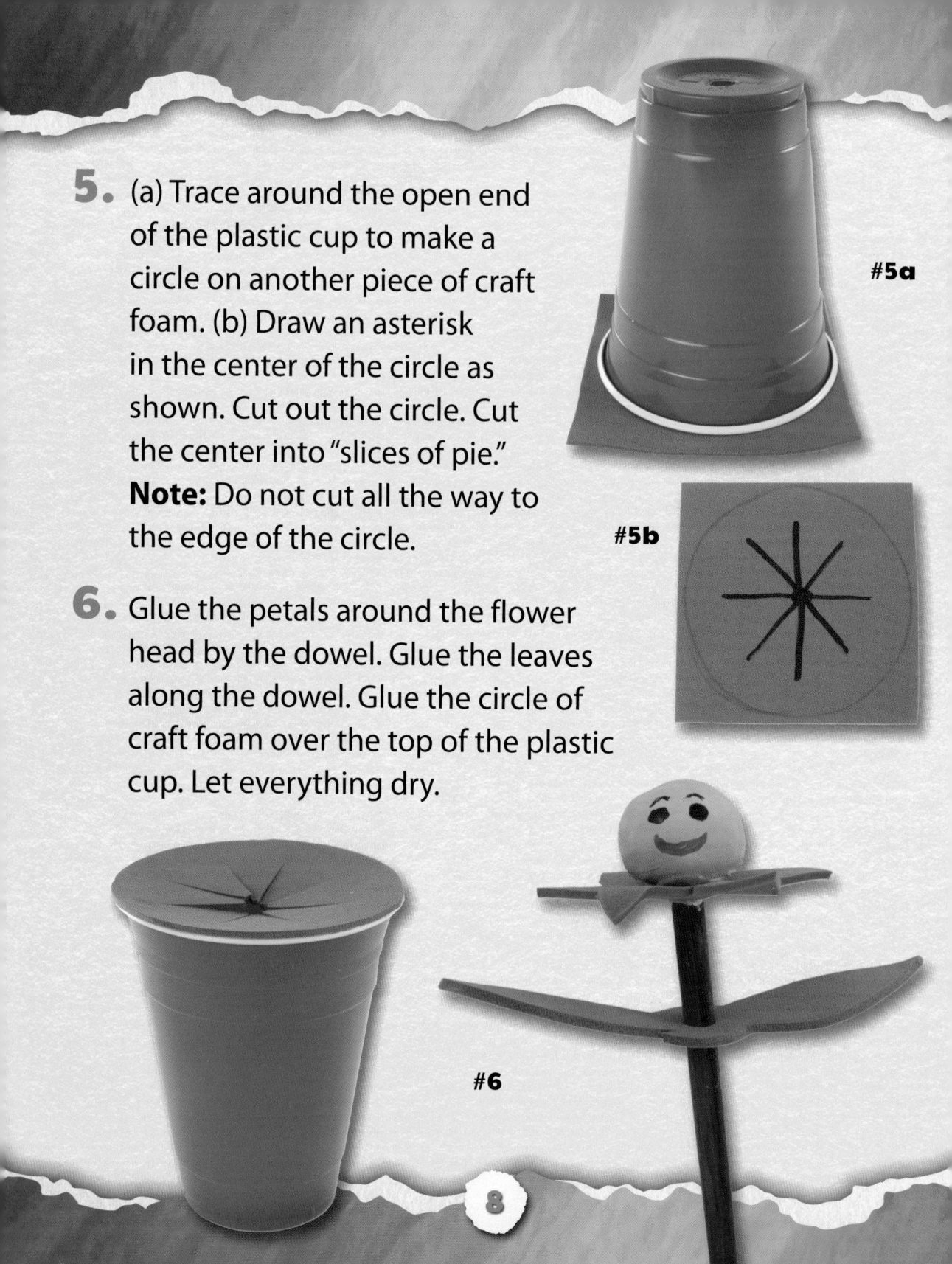

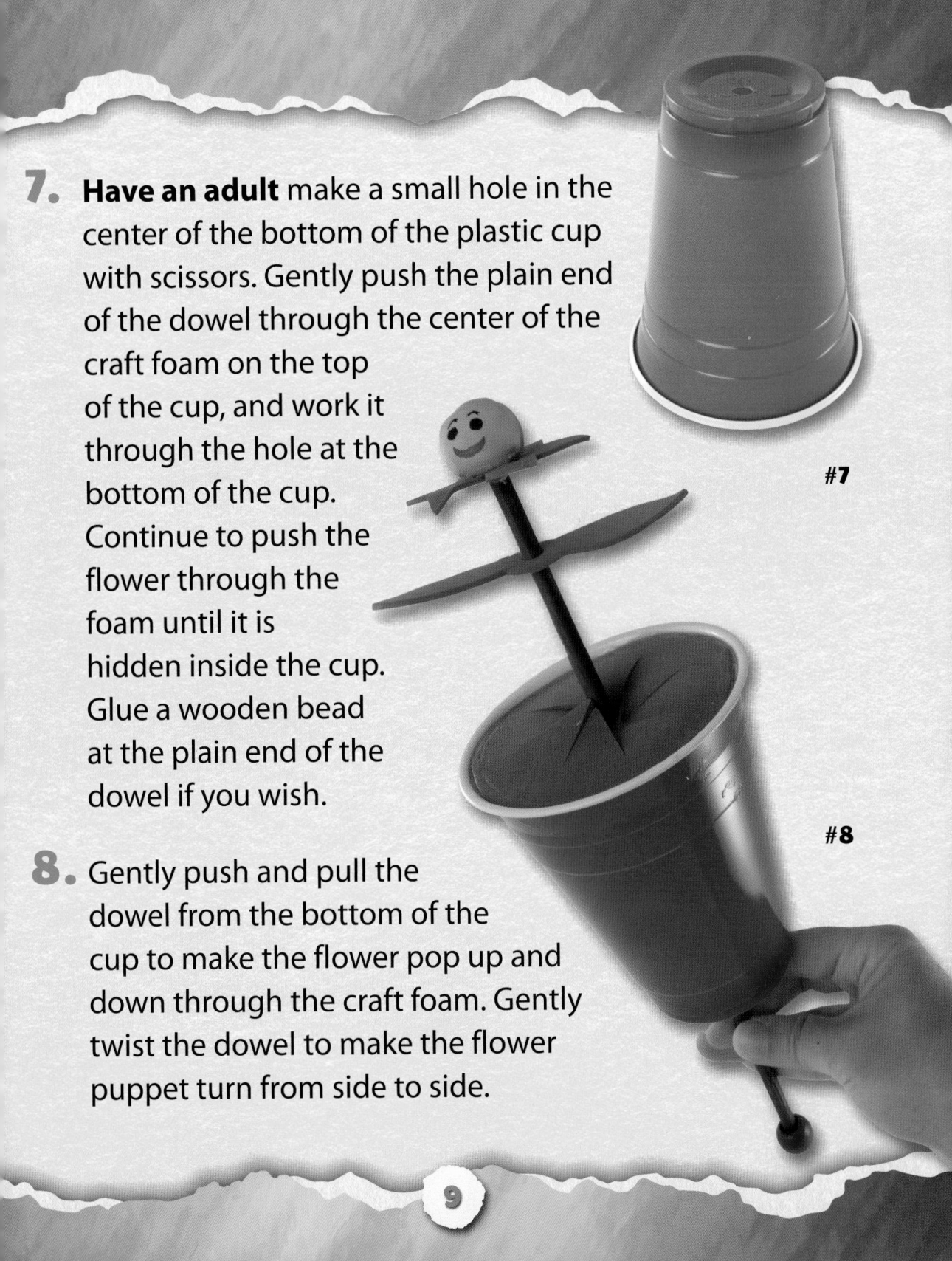

7. **Have an adult** make a small hole in the center of the bottom of the plastic cup with scissors. Gently push the plain end of the dowel through the center of the craft foam on the top of the cup, and work it through the hole at the bottom of the cup. Continue to push the flower through the foam until it is hidden inside the cup. Glue a wooden bead at the plain end of the dowel if you wish.

#7

8. Gently push and pull the dowel from the bottom of the cup to make the flower pop up and down through the craft foam. Gently twist the dowel to make the flower puppet turn from side to side.

#8

BUNNY MASK

The Germans had myths about Eostre (pronounced "Ee-stray"), the goddess of spring. She would send her speedy messenger, a bunny, to deliver eggs so people would know spring was on its way. The word *Easter* is based on the goddess's name. Germans that came to the United States brought their customs and symbols for celebrating Easter, such as bunnies and eggs. This bunny mask is fun for celebrating Easter or just hopping around in the spring sunshine!

WHAT YOU WILL NEED:

- scissors
- pencil or permanent markers
- craft foam—one sheet, 9 x 12 inches, any color
- pieces of craft foam in many colors (optional)
- glue
- yarn—two 6-inch pieces
- duct tape (optional)

WHAT TO DO:

1. Print and cut out the bunny mask pattern from page 45. Use a pencil or marker to trace it onto the sheet of craft foam.

#1

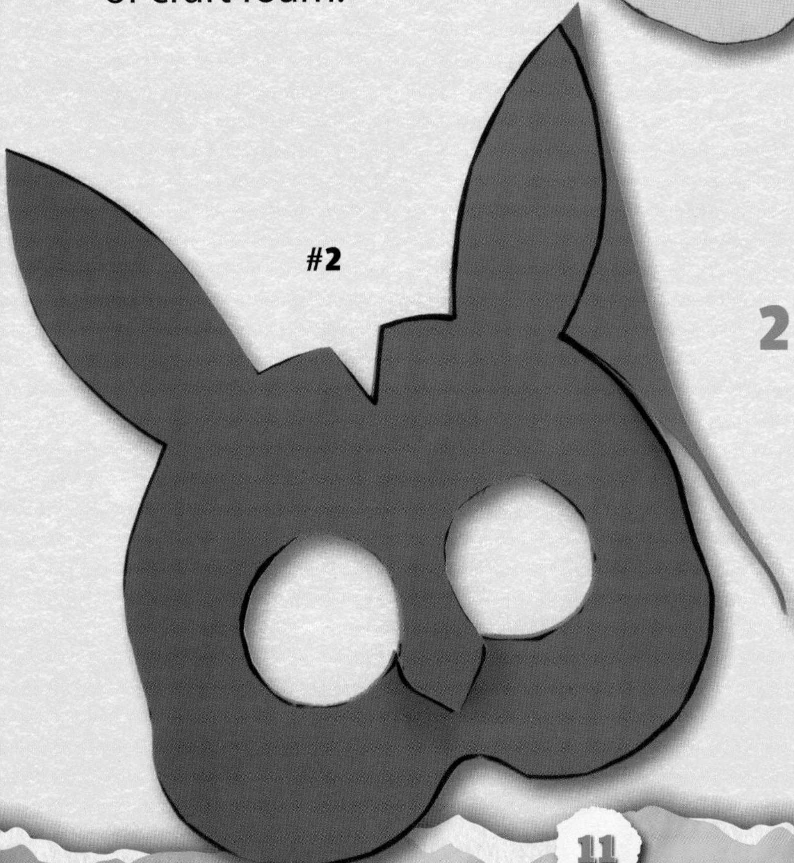

#2

2. Cut out the pattern.

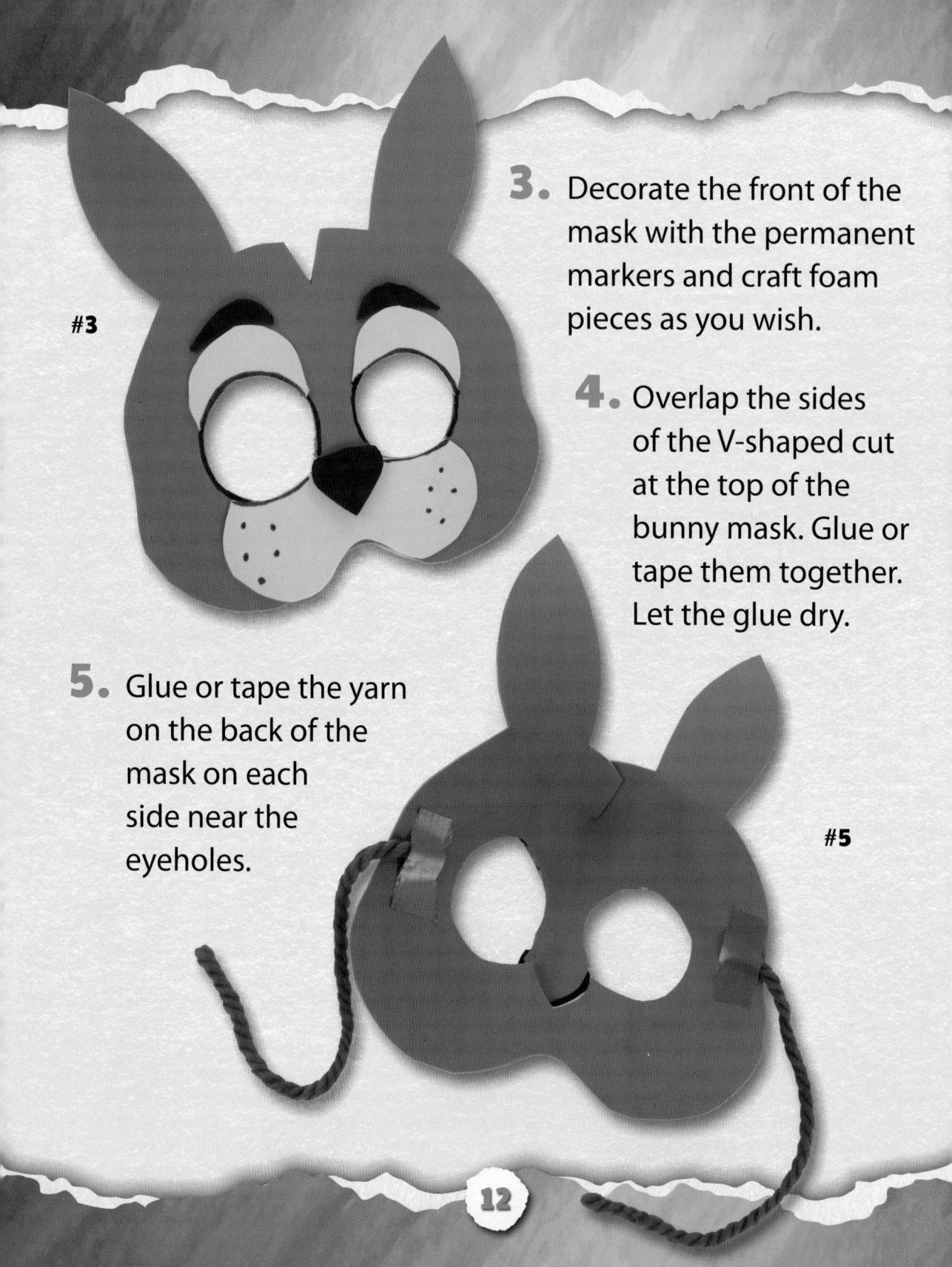

#3

3. Decorate the front of the mask with the permanent markers and craft foam pieces as you wish.

4. Overlap the sides of the V-shaped cut at the top of the bunny mask. Glue or tape them together. Let the glue dry.

5. Glue or tape the yarn on the back of the mask on each side near the eyeholes.

#5

6. Gently place the mask on your face and tie the yarn behind your head so that it fits comfortably.

Baby Bird Clothespin Puppet

In spring, birds migrate, which means they change the area where they live. They fly from their winter homes in the Southern Hemisphere to areas in the Northern Hemisphere where there is more food. When it is spring in the north, it is fall in the south. The birds build nests and lay eggs. Chicks break out of the eggs and cry for food. The birds feed their chicks insects and worms.

What you will need:

- scissors
- pencil or permanent markers
- craft foam—different colors
- modeling material
- a spring-type clothespin
- craft stick
- glue
- feathers, beads, craft eyes (optional)
- watercolor paints
- paintbrush

WHAT TO DO:

1. Print and cut out the patterns on page 42. Trace two copies of each part onto craft foam with a pencil or marker. Cut them out.

#1

2. Use the modeling material to make a ball about the size of a grape and another ball about the size of a walnut.

#2

3. Shape the grape-sized ball of modeling material around the top of the clothespin near the clasping end to look like a chick's head.

4. Shape the walnut-sized ball of modeling material around the underside of the clothespin to make the body.

5. While the material is still soft, use the craft stick to make slots for the wings and feet. Stick the wings and feet into the slots until they stay.

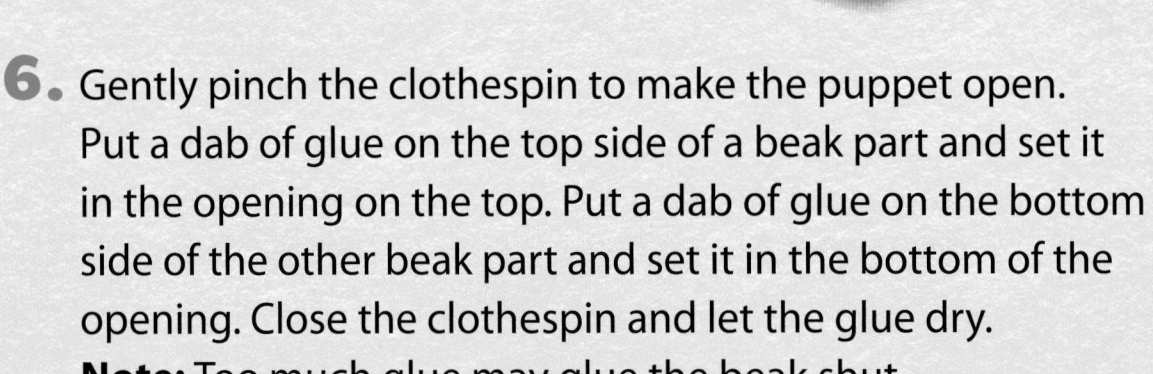

#5

6. Gently pinch the clothespin to make the puppet open. Put a dab of glue on the top side of a beak part and set it in the opening on the top. Put a dab of glue on the bottom side of the other beak part and set it in the bottom of the opening. Close the clothespin and let the glue dry.
Note: Too much glue may glue the beak shut.

#6

7. Glue on beads or craft eyes and feathers. Use watercolors as you wish. Let the puppet dry.

8. Gently squeeze the open end of the clothespin to make the baby bird open and close its beak.

#7

Movable Duck Picture

When people want to travel long distances, they use a highway. When ducks want to travel long distances, they use a "flyway." That is what scientists call the routes that ducks take in the spring to their northern homes and in the fall to their southern homes. Ducks live in wetlands. They have oily skin and feathers that make the water roll off them when they swim. Here is a happy duck who loves the spring rain!

What you will need:

- scissors
- pencil
- three sheets of card stock
- crayons or markers
- blue cellophane (optional)
- paper fastener
- glue
- craft feathers (optional)

1. Print and cut out the patterns from pages 42 and 43. Use a pencil or marker to trace them onto two sheets of card stock.

#1

2. Decorate the duck and the background with crayons, markers, or pieces of blue cellophane as you wish.

3. Cut out the duck along the solid black outline. Be careful not to cut off the long paper handle connected to the duck's body.

#3, #4

4. Cut along the solid black lines of the background sheet.

5. Slip the long handle on the duck's body through the slit in the background sheet. Push it all the way through to the curved opening on the side.

#5

6. Push a paper fastener through the middle of the duck and through the background sheet. Set it in place.

#6

7. Decorate the duck with craft feathers as you wish. Hide the paper fastener with some feathers. **Note:** Do not put glue right on the head of the paper fastener as it might keep it from moving as it should.

8. Put a little glue around the edges of the back side of the background sheet and set it evenly on the third sheet of card stock to finish. Let it dry. Gently move the handle up and down to make the duck splash in the puddle.

#8

Garden Plant Sticks

Spring is a great time to plant seeds for flowers, fruits, and vegetables! Plant seeds when the chance of frost is gone. Have an adult help you prepare a grow box or garden space. Remove any weeds from the planting area. Lay the seeds in rows and cover them with just a little soil. Plant the seeds where they will receive a lot of sunshine. Some plants, such as sweet peas, broccoli, carrots, and beets, like the cool temperatures of early spring. Other plants, such as corn, beans, and tomatoes, need more sun and the warmer temperatures of late spring.

Once the seeds are in the ground, how will you remember what you planted and where? With these garden plant sticks!

What you will need:

- ❀ scissors
- ❀ pencil or permanent markers
- ❀ craft foam—different colors
- ❀ acrylic paints
- ❀ a large craft stick or wooden paint paddle (found in hardware stores and paint stores)
- ❀ paintbrush
- ❀ glue

WHAT TO DO:

1. Print and cut out the vegetable patterns on page 44. Use pencil or marker to trace them onto the craft foam. Or you can design your own patterns for the plants you are planting.

#1

2. Cut out the patterns from the craft foam.

3. Paint the craft stick or paint paddle. Let it dry.

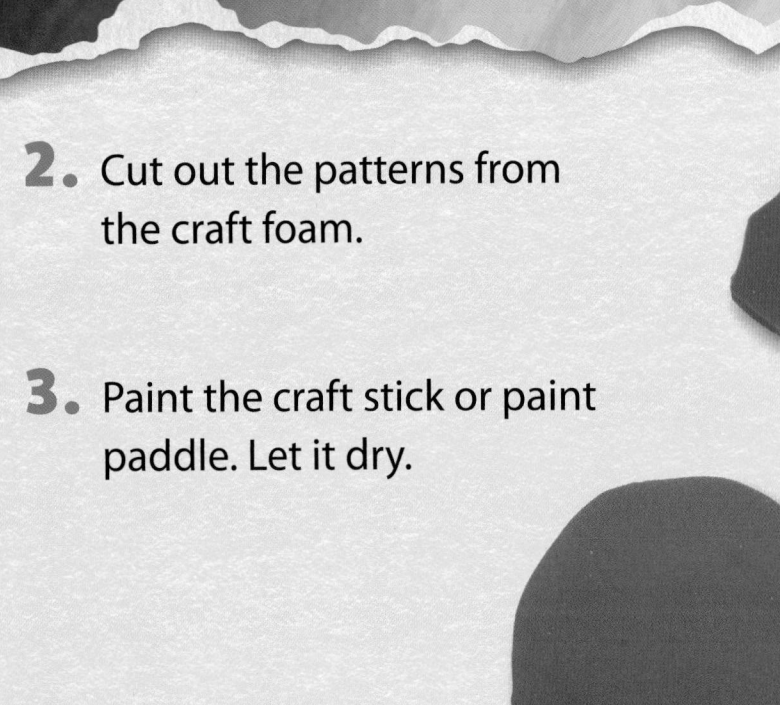

#3

4. Glue the pattern piece to one end of the stick. Let the glue dry.

5. Use a marker to write the name of the plant on the stick.

6. Gently push the stick into the soil next to where you planted the seeds of the plant shown on the stick.

#5

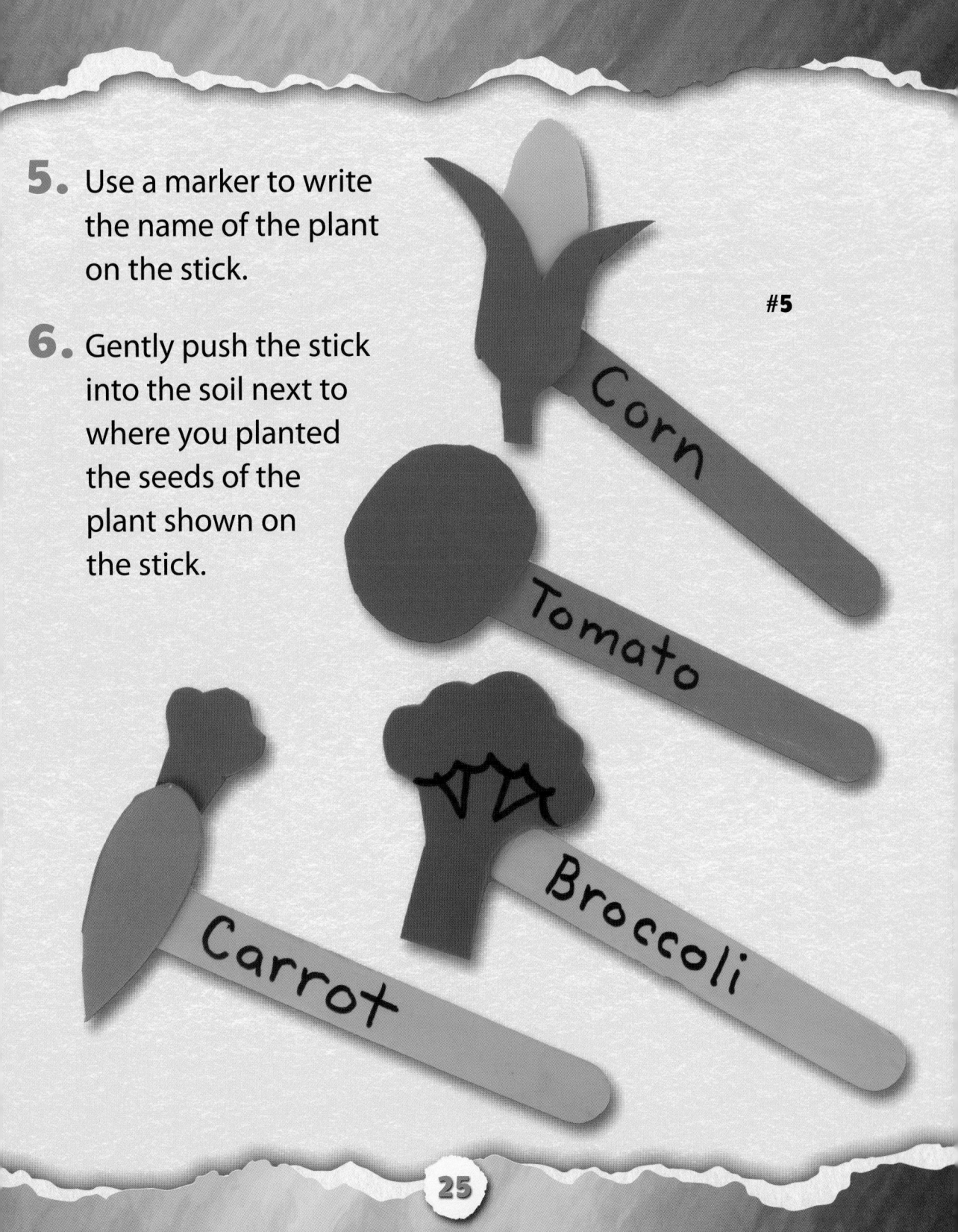

Corn

Tomato

Broccoli

Carrot

LEPRECHAUN JUMPING JACK

Green is the color of spring and the color of St. Patrick's Day, the holiday of the patron saint of Ireland. The Irish have tales about little fairy folk called leprechauns. They are quick-witted, quick-tempered, and quick on their feet! They have magical powers and can grant wishes, if a human is clever enough to capture one. They traditionally dress in green clothes with a vest and top hat. A jumping jack is a jointed puppet that dances when its string is pulled.

WHAT YOU WILL NEED:

- ❀ scissors
- ❀ pencil
- ❀ light cardboard
- ❀ crayons or markers
- ❀ a hole punch
- ❀ string
- ❀ paper fasteners
- ❀ a bead—plastic or wood, about the size of a large pea

WHAT TO DO:

1. Print and cut out the patterns of the leprechaun and all the parts from page 43. Use pencil or marker to trace them onto the light cardboard.

#1

#3

2. Decorate the leprechaun and the different parts with markers or crayons as you wish.

3. Cut the pattern out of the light cardboard.

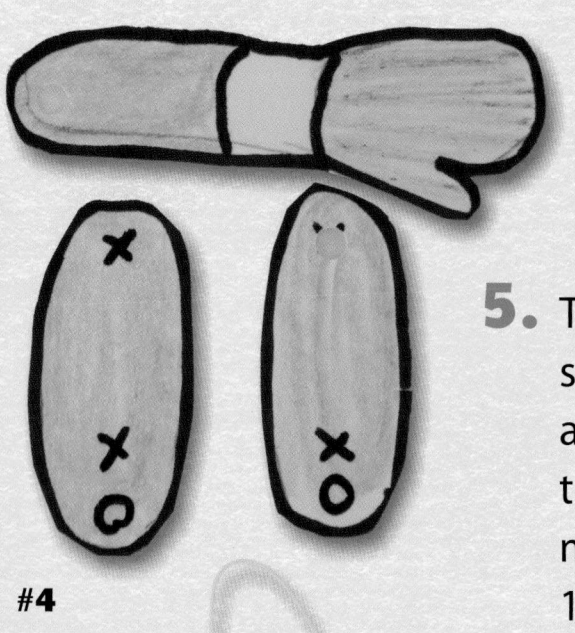

#4

4. Use a hole punch to make holes where the Os and Xs are marked on the pattern.

5. Tie a 7-inch-long piece of string to the tops of the arms and one through the legs, through each hole that was marked with an "O." Tie a 10- to 12-inch-long string through the hole in the top of the head.

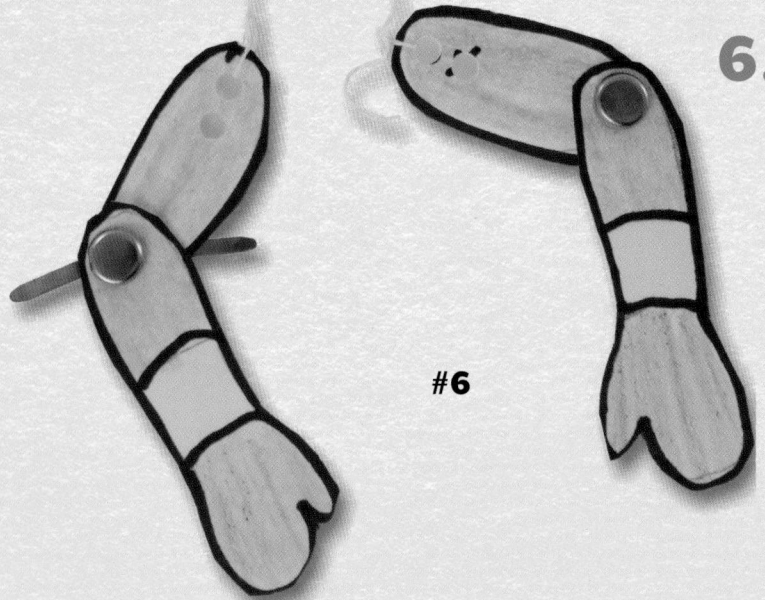

#6

6. Put a paper fastener through each hole that was marked with an X. Fasten the arms together at the elbows and the legs together at the knees. Fasten the limbs to the body.

#7

#8

7. Fasten a 14-inch-long string to the short strings connecting the arms and legs. Tie the bead on the end of the string.

8. Hang on to the string at the top of the leprechaun and gently tug on the bead to make the leprechaun's arms and legs swing and jump.

PASSOVER "FOUR QUESTIONS" LAMP

More than 3,300 years ago, the Jewish people were slaves to the Egyptians. Ten plagues (disasters) happened in Egypt at that time. The Jewish slaves followed the directions of their leader Moses so that the plagues would pass over their people. The Jews then left Egypt as quickly as they could, taking only foods they could eat in a hurry. The Jewish people celebrate their freedom from slavery with a holiday called Passover. It is celebrated in the Hebrew month of Nisan, which is during the months of March and April.

During a Passover meal, an adult asks the people at the table, "Why is this night different from all other nights?"

The youngest child will then ask these four questions when the food is served:

"On all other nights, we eat either unleavened or leavened bread, but tonight we eat only unleavened bread?

On all other nights, we eat all kinds of vegetables and herbs, but tonight we eat only bitter herbs?

On all other nights, we do not dip our vegetables in salt water, but tonight we dip them twice?

On all other nights, we eat either sitting or reclining, but tonight we only recline?"

WHAT YOU WILL NEED:

- 🌸 scissors
- 🌸 pencil
- 🌸 card stock
- 🌸 crayons or markers
- 🌸 glue

- 🌸 tracing paper
- 🌸 cellophane tape
- 🌸 a small battery-operated light (or tea light)

WHAT TO DO:

1. Print the patterns from pages 38, 39, and 40. Only cut out the areas outlined in solid black lines. Trace the three patterns onto card stock.

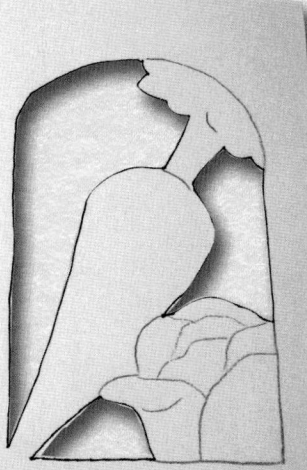

#1

2. Decorate the images. Remember to only cut out the areas outlined in solid black lines.

#3

3. Glue tracing paper to the backs of the decorated card stock sheets. Trim the tracing paper if needed.

4. Fold the card stock sheets in half so that the short sides meet.

5. Tape the long edges of the card stock sheets together to form an open-ended box.

#5

6. On the top piece of the lamp, write the question, "Why is this night different from all others?"

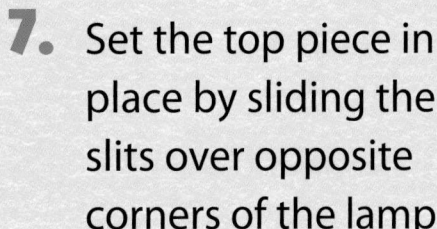

#7

7. Set the top piece in place by sliding the slits over opposite corners of the lamp.

8. Turn on the battery-operated light and place it on the table. Put the lamp over it.

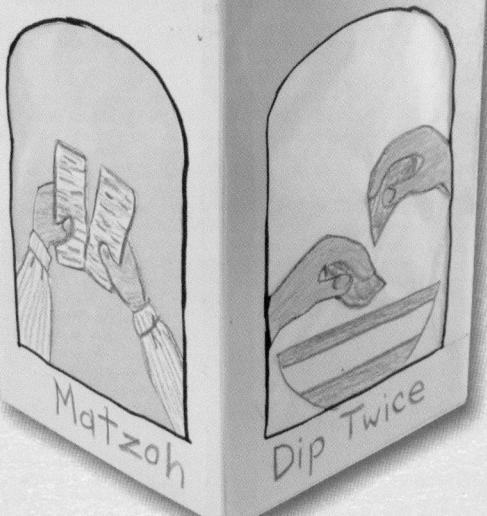

#8

Mother's Day or Father's Day "Big Hug" Trick Card

Mother's Day and Father's Day are celebrated in spring and summer in many countries. Anna Jarvis started a letter-writing campaign in the early 1900s to encourage setting a national day to honor mothers. On May 9, 1914, President Woodrow Wilson announced that the second Sunday of May was a holiday to honor mothers in the United States. Sonora Smart Dodd soon campaigned for a national holiday for fathers. It was not until 1966 that the third Sunday in June was set as an official holiday for honoring fathers in the United States.

What you will need:

- scissors
- pencil
- card stock
- crayons, colored pencils, or markers
- construction paper— 9 x 12 inches
- glue

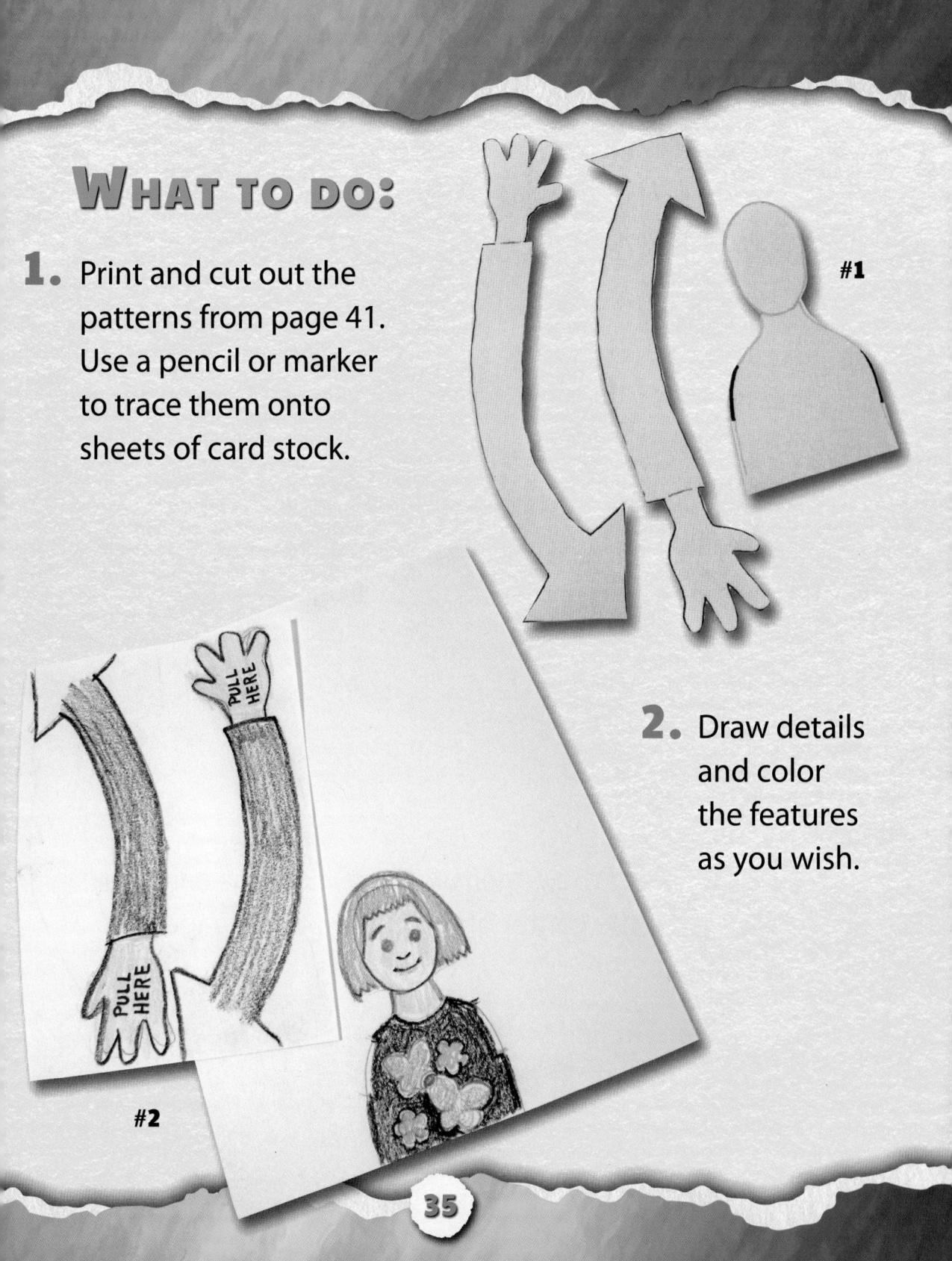

WHAT TO DO:

1. Print and cut out the patterns from page 41. Use a pencil or marker to trace them onto sheets of card stock.

#1

2. Draw details and color the features as you wish.

PULL HERE

PULL HERE

PULL HERE

#2

3. Cut out the arms. Only cut along the solid black slits on the body. This is the base of the card.

4. Fold in the points on the end of the arms. Insert the arms through the slits in the body. Unfold the points once they are through the slits.

PULL HERE

#4

5. Put glue around the edges on the back of the card stock and glue it to the center of the construction paper.

6. Fold the card in half so that the short sides meet. Gently slide the arms into the slits of the card.

7. Write a message on the front of the card and on the inside. Be sure to sign your name!

#8

8. When the card is opened, the hands can be pulled gently out to each side to make them stretch.

PATTERNS

The percentages included on the patterns tell you how much to enlarge or shrink the image using a copier. Most copiers and printers have an adjustable size/percentage feature to change the size of an image when you print it. After you print the pattern to its correct size, cut it out. Trace it onto the material listed in the craft.

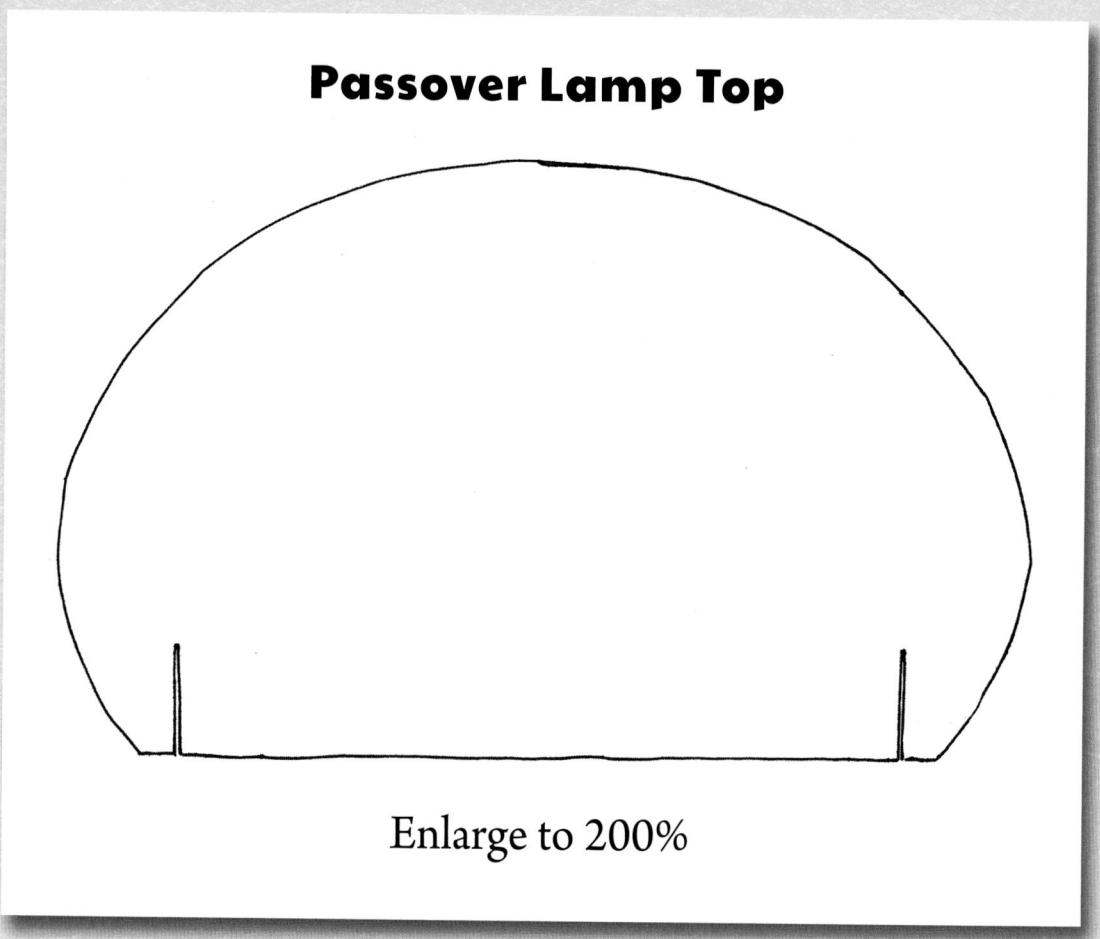

Passover Lamp Top

Enlarge to 200%

Passover Lamp A

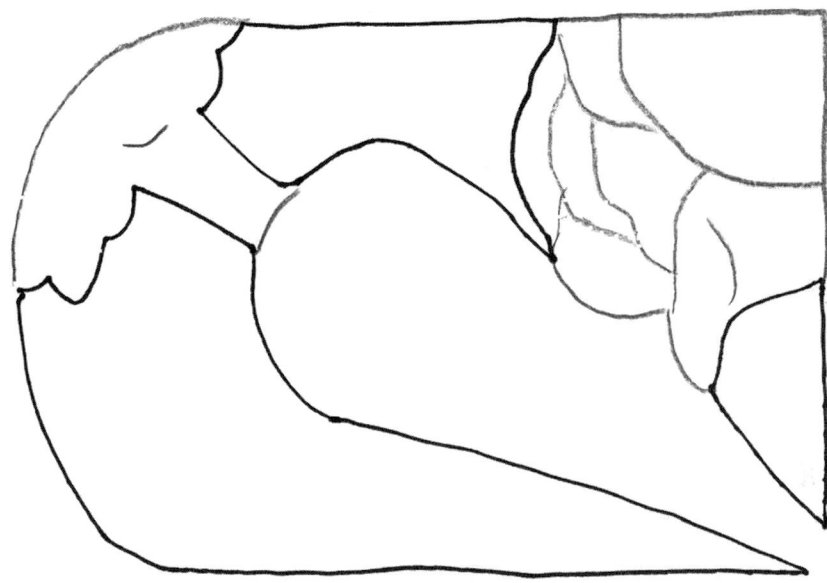

Enlarge to 140%

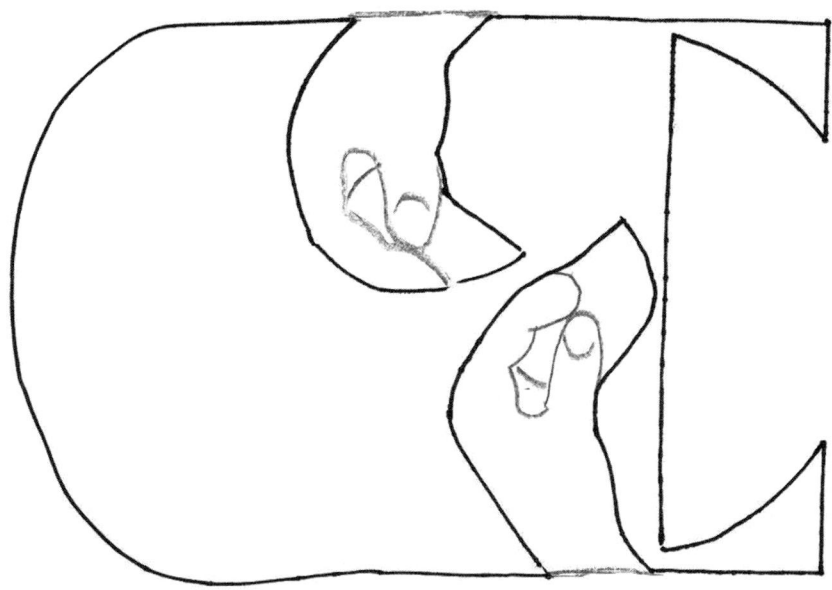

Passover Lamp B

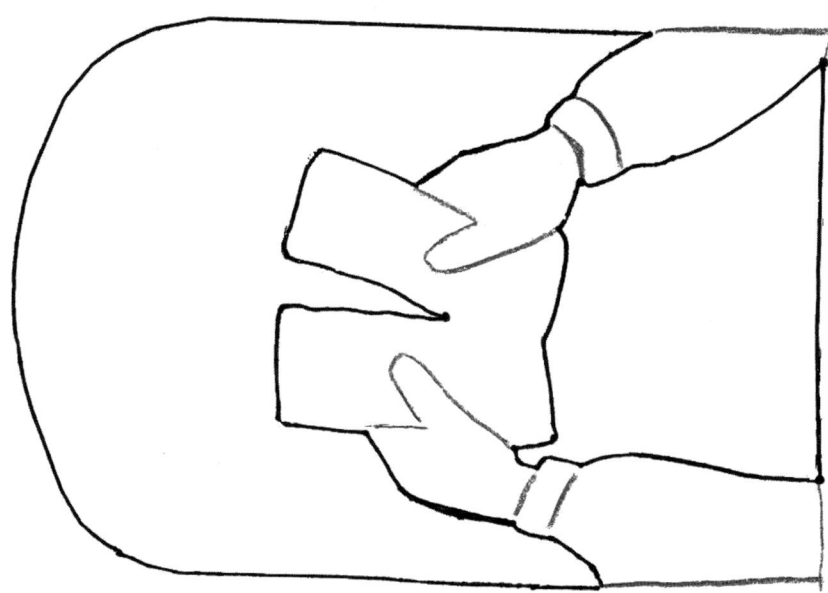

Enlarge to 140%

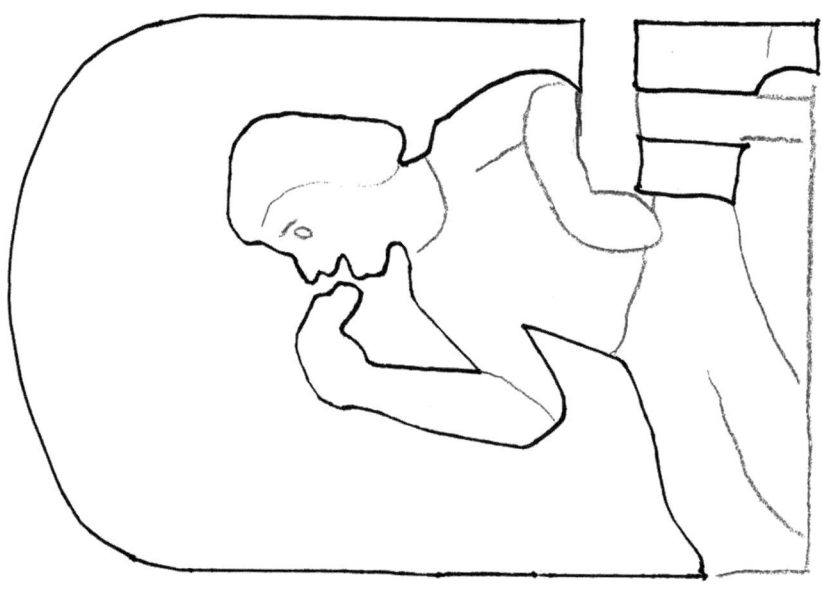

"Big Hug" Card Arms

Enlarge to 200%

"Big Hug" Card Base

Enlarge to 200%

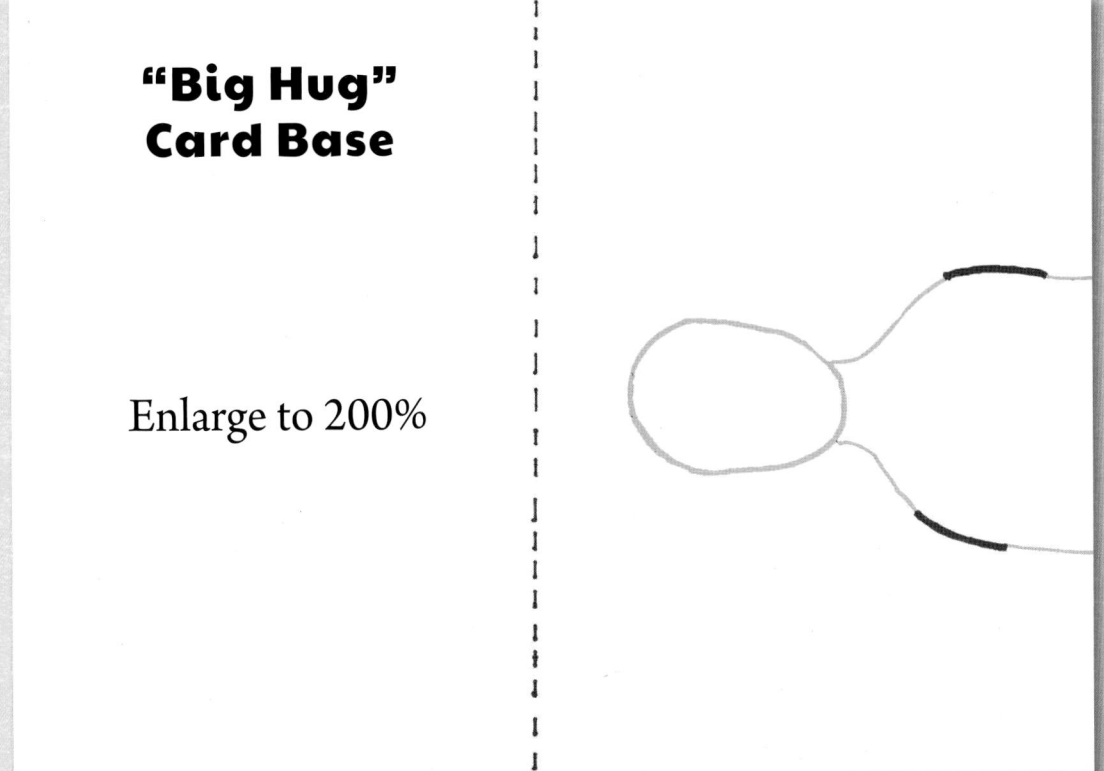

Movable Duck

Enlarge to 150%

Clothespin Bird (cut 2 of each)

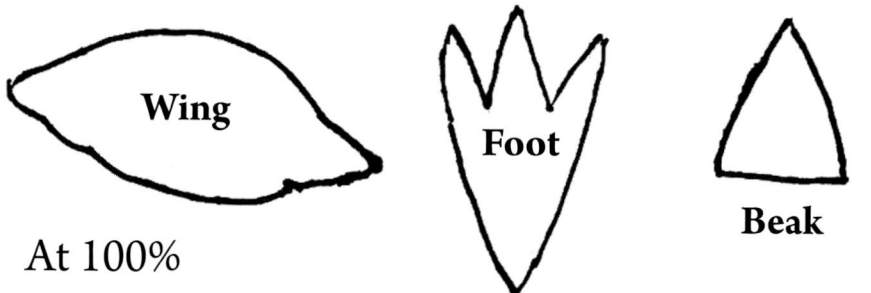

Wing

Foot

Beak

At 100%

Enlarge to 200%

Leprechaun Jumping Jack

Movable Duck Base

Enlarge to 300%

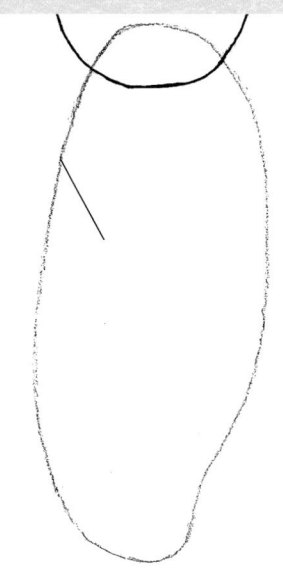

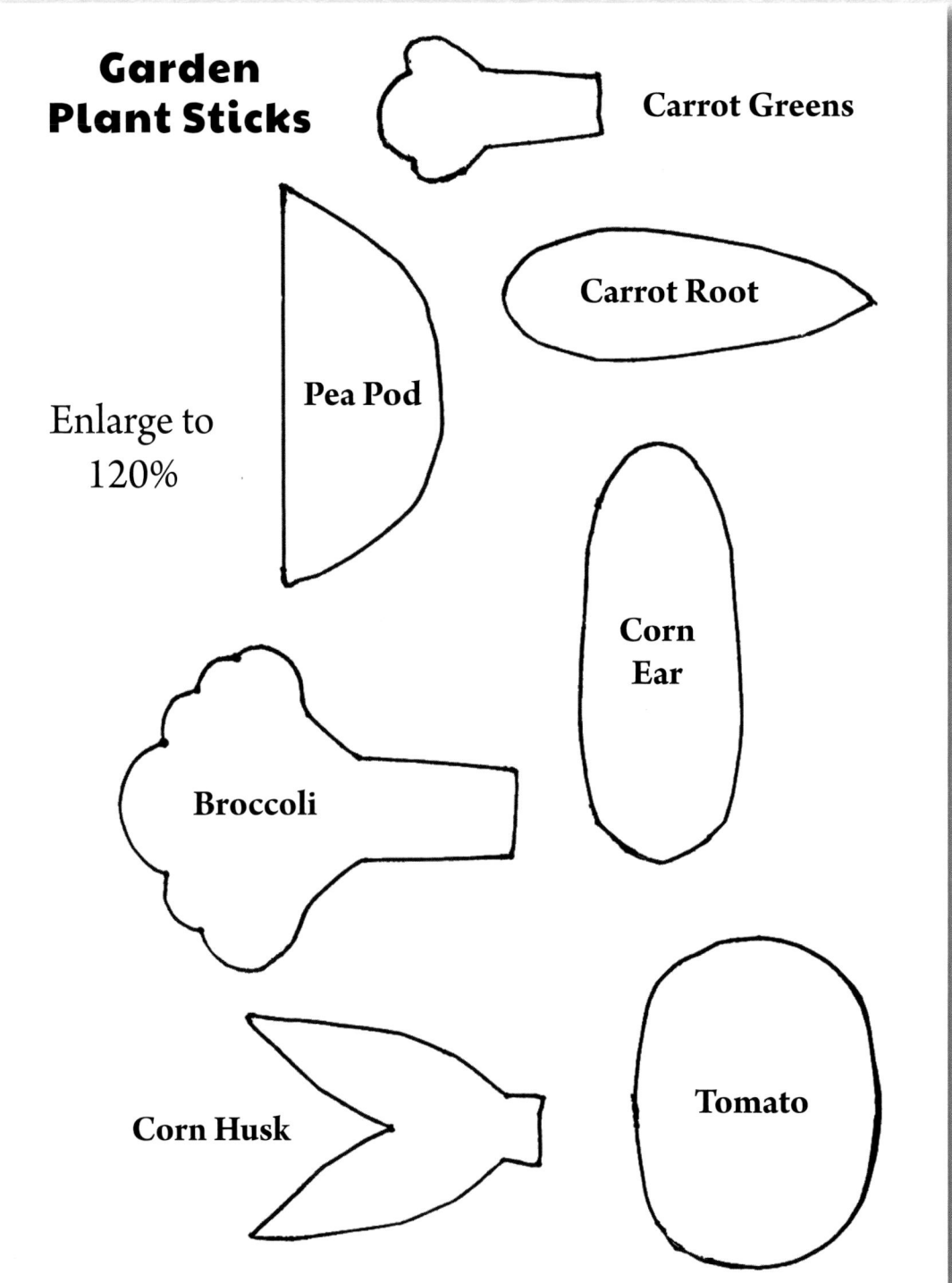

Garden Plant Sticks

Carrot Greens

Carrot Root

Pea Pod

Enlarge to 120%

Corn Ear

Broccoli

Corn Husk

Tomato

Bunny Mask

Enlarge to 165%

READ ABOUT

Books

Biddle, Steve, and Megumi Biddle. *Make Your Own Greeting Cards.* Mineola, N.Y.: Dover Publications, 2013.

LeBaron, Marie. *Make and Takes for Kids: 50 Crafts Throughout the Year.* Hoboken, N.J.: John Wiley & Sons, Inc., 2012.

Internet Addresses

Spoonful: Spring Crafts

http://spoonful.com/spring/spring-crafts

Activity Village: Spring Crafts

http://www.activityvillage.co.uk/spring-crafts

Visit Randel McGee's Web site at
http://www.mcgeeproductions.com

INDEX

About the Author

Randel McGee has liked to make things and has played with paper and scissors as long as he can remember. He also likes telling stories and performing. He is an internationally recognized storyteller, ventriloquist, and puppeteer. He and his dragon puppet, Groark, have performed all around the United States and Asia and have appeared in two award-winning video series on character education. He also portrays the famous author Hans Christian Andersen in storytelling performances, where he makes amazing cut-paper designs while he tells stories, just like Andersen did. He likes showing teachers and children the fun they can have with paper projects, storytelling, and puppetry. Randel McGee lives in central California with his wife, Marsha. They have five grown children.